Cloves
& Honey

Cloves
& Honey

love poems

Athena Kildegaard

NODIN PRESS

Cover painting: "Summer Afternoon Jasmine" by Michael Eble
Design and layout: John Toren

ISBN: 978-1-935666-36-3
Library of Congress Cataloging-in-Publication Data
Kildegaard, Athena, 1959-
Cloves & honey : love poems / Athena Kildegaard.
p. cm.
Includes bibliographical references and index.
ISBN 978-1-935666-36-3 (alk. paper)
I. Title. II. Title: Cloves and honey.
PS3611.I4496C56 2012
811'.6--dc23
                    2011049217

Thanks to the Lake Region Arts Council for the LRAC/McKnight Fellowship—and for their faith in this project.

Thanks to Margaret Hasse whose keen eye, honey-sweet generosity, and fearlessness are unmatched. Thanks to Dara Syrkin who saw the crazy love and passed it on. 'At dinner with friends' is for Debra and John. 'For merriment' is for Dennis and Carole. 'In a preface to a book of love' is for Beatrice and Ashley. 'In what remained of an Augustinian monastery' is for Lise and Luther. 'My father took pictures' is for Pop. 'On his fiftieth birthday, Issa wrote: From now on' is for Cheryl and Lawrence. 'Otter was the first lover' is for Carol. 'When I'm with you, yellow' is for Beatrice and Paul. The little ones are for Margaret K. And 'In our house of love' is for all our friends and family: in your houses we've found love. And special thanks to family, friends, and a few strangers who received a love poem every day in 2010. You strengthened my resolve.

Nodin Press
530 N 3rd Street
Suite 120
Mpls, MN,
55401

to Arne, *mi alma, mi vida*

And to Lawrence & Kathleen and Axel & Fylla,
for showing us how good it can be

Spring

Why this impulse to write about love?

Close your eyes
it is not dark
in your imagination

say crow
and there's flight

say wave
and jellyfish tremble

chickadee, and black shells
of sunflower seeds float down
to where a beetle tight-wires
across the grass

What is this claim we make
over and over,
love, love

the persistence
of the silver maple
squirrels high-wiring

close your eyes
say love
that's a bee

live-wired in the blossom

Hafiz says
Love is the great work
though every heart is first
an apprentice.
I hope to be an apprentice
all my life. There's joy
in bumbling.
Why should I know
already, or even in twenty years,
just what to say, when to take
your hand, when to lean close
to kiss your lower lip, when
to close my mouth. Love
is not mastery.
Come now, let's practice!

Some days I'm inclined
to follow you like a five-
year-old. Whatcha doing?
What's that? How come?

I'm inclined toward you
as a morning glory, a willow
on the prairie's edge. As
sun in late afternoon

stretching shadows wacky thin.
Your incline is my desire. Mine
your steady horizon. I'm following
you to see what matters.

The palm of my hand
knows the watermelon's cool arc,
an infant's elbow cresting,
the restful cat's back.
The palm of my hand
knows how to smoothe a sheet,
to lift itself into the day,
how to pull up the night
and settle against the sure
repose of your waist.

There is that in me which reaches
for you no matter the hour, no
matter how far or near you are.

There is that confidence mornings
when robins try the warming air
and that humbling whirr of moths

against the screen. Whatever in me
reaches out carries with it every
morning a rejuvenation, the damp

pushing up of rhubarb, deer in
the dew passing their soft lips
over grass. There is that in me, too,

the freshness, when I reach for you,
my mind brave as leaves
before the unfurling.

Some days whatever you say—
    does this button match
        we have enough rhubarb

I listen not so much to the words
    the dictionary meanings
        the syllables

no, what I hear is how you
    are the same person as yesterday
        muscle, timbre, synapse.

Once we sat on the floor under one blanket,
your hand down my shirt,
three of your friends on the couch cheering Guy Lafleur,

And one morning, eighth floor above 53rd, you woke up talking
an alarm soared toward the lake
Harold the neon butcher chopped chopped at a running chicken

And yellow roses & honey mead on the fold-down table of our
                                     VW camper van
parked on the banks of Agua Azul
where a black and dangerous snake floated by as I washed my hair
                                              in the water

And sleeping through an ice storm, both children between us in bed
ourselves the only source of heat
we reached for one another across their tender fetal bodies

And writing limericks for Elgin & Belvedere & Beloit as we drove,
you peeled grapes, fed them to me
how we could have been anywhere your thumb balanced on my
                                              lower lip.

¹ Or *couch*, in other regions; for a curious and probing search into the role of the sofa as a centerpiece of the living room or front room see *From Chaise to Faint* by the noted historian of interior spaces, M. A. Sallonne

² The history of the phrase is clouded in mystery, but there is no doubt that when the French arrived in Britain they were considered too-worldly, crass, sexually unrestrained, and lacking in propriety

³ The tongue has long been considered an organ of foolishness

⁴ We do not have the space here to explore the distinctions inherent in the words *love* and *lust* so the determined reader is advised to search her own heart for insight into these distinctions

⁵ No, consult not the heart for it is fickle and besides we've gotten over those pre-Renaissance notions of the bodily functions being somehow reflective of the unpredictable emotions; systems such as the digestive or circulatory cannot be confused with metaphors for lust and love

⁶ See Marvell, Andrew, "amorous birds of prey . . ."

⁷ These passages were cut from the original by the editor of the first edition as being "turpitudinous" but were gratefully reintroduced in this new illustrated edition

Finches twine in sunlight—
all the world's agog.

꣠

Sheer a sheep and it shivers—
that's how it feels,
love.

꣠

Chickadees chirrup
in the pines. Damp like parted lips—
this morning eden.

꣠

Every day the muezzins
chant across the Sea of Marmara.
Every day: love, love, love!

꣠

The first time—
my fingertip from your shoulder to your nipple—
wave coming in, wave going out.

There must be rules for what goes
into a love poem: a full moon, a red rose,

breast—heaving or cream-pale—night
and stars, a balcony, all that seems right,

and a trellis precariously tipped against
a cold wall where the lover, alert and tensed

can wait until the moon and stars have set
and in the quiet heave himself up and get

over the crenelated wall to where—
no, this is silly, I can't go there—

we're fifty after all, do mostly what we should,
follow no known rules, though heaving's good.

In our house of love
the doors open both directions.
On a windy day
the weathervane, a bronze rooster
with a hollow belly, stirs up music reedy
and primal. Everyone we know
is here. We run out into dandelions
and cottonwood fluff.
When the wind dies down
those who aren't daydreaming
wander back into the house.
Some carry up jars from
the spidery basement, jars
of pickled lemons and salted figs,
a waxed wheel of aged cheddar,
bottles of cider with cork stoppers.
Our son hauls from the attic
the cedar trunk with *Destination:*
Paradise burned into the lid.
Out of it our daughter brings honey-gold scarves,
Panama hats with poems in yellow ink
slipped into the band, black fur stoles,
a man's wool full-torso swimming suit,
postcards from the border, a banjo, an accordion.
The daydreamers awaken
and come into the house smelling of dusk.
The doors stand open right through the night.

Standing below the crabapple thick with pink blooms
I'm sure I can see the outline of the green heron
who called and called last year for a mate.

How many of these primordial birds can live
out here on the altered prairie? Sure enough she answered
and they went about the business of guaranteeing

the future and we skirted the tree with binoculars
to mark their patient progress: nest, awkward shifting
from branch to branch, a pair of ogle-eyed chicks,

and then abandonment. If they don't come this year
or next, can anything be as certain as it was then?

A scientist on the radio
said you can enter a black hole

but you can never get out.
It's the dark fairy tale

of the universe. All day
I carried the brief story

around with me, turning
it for some metaphor

about love. Wishing to say
to you: may your love

be a black hole. And that
would be enough

except for how scary it is.
That falling.

The wind asks
the tree: how long
will you stand
here, in my arms?

The tree throws
back its head
and says:
when will you
let go?

Enough of writing about love. Who, really,
wants to hear about this, day in, day out,
as if it were all that really mattered.

A tree on fourth street, what was it, elm? or
ash? spilled its pollen in one wind and so,
a perfectly lineated puddle of yellow

lay there, sidewalk, grass, curb, all gold,
a sphere of fertility that knows only
the boundary of leaf. The sun reflected

on the earth's surface: a good metaphor.
Or the fallen desires of the world. Or
a coin, payment for another strophe of love.

If we lived in a village
of a few hundred souls,
a few hundred sturdy bodies
calloused and sun-worn,
in short houses with wavy windows,
red hollyhocks touching the thatch,
we'd wear wool
close to our skin, we'd carry
water and tease in the cow
when winter blew over,
we'd wake to frost on the coverlet
and we'd hesitate, hold one another
before rising, before chores,
without speaking a word,
the warmth between us—
like cloves and honey—
a private delight.

Slender moon white as pinion—
geese land in pairs
on the silver water.

❧

Maple seeds flutter earthward—
inside I play Mendelssohn—
songs without words.

❧

Grass tickles the bee's belly.
What else can we listen for
this spring morning?

❧

The iron of your heart
levers me open.

Hafiz says *Beloved, drink the wine.*

A wood duck stands on the lowest branch.
It would never think to leap up,
like a squirrel.

A little tipsiness, says the Sufi master,
takes us closer to god.

The wood duck stands utterly balanced,
its webbed feet sufficient
for the time.

I'm not an animist, maybe not even a believer,
but I have faith
in the duck.

Here, love, pour the wine!

Along the coast
past Bogalusa a grebe
cannot catch her breath
so clogged she is by oil.

Dandelions open everywhere.
We're still wearing sweaters.
All those shore birds,
the calving dolphins,

oyster beds now black.
A wind moves the grass,
my mind cannot settle.
Love is a luxury, I think.

The young boxelder
has only male flowers.
Years later, older and thicker,
it blooms female.
And for a space of time,
even on the same branch,
both blossom.
(All these years you've been he,
I've been she.)
Wind twines
the boxelder's branches,
the song sparrow's
nest. Red–winged blackbirds
sing high up,
a song full of wild abandon.

Humpback whales sing their low
songs of love, long waves of tone
moving through their salty world
farther than we can walk
in a day, in several days. How
beautiful to tell your love to mollusks
and anemones, the floating rays,
shy octopus, the jellyfish
bioluminescing below the surface
where cloud shadows bend
and fold from chariot to fan
to trailing ribbon of silk
until they thin to nothing
and still the whale sings.

Kittiwakes skim waves
that lap toward a glacier
beside sheer angles of granite—
gray beside the eerie blue of ice,
blue of eons, gray of eons.

Here we are our whole selves,
moving like the birds
toward what endures,
toward one another,
incremental and necessary.

Summer

Every night we travel
apart, find ourselves
in the dioramas
of dream. You slowly lift
right off the ground,
wingless and borne
among pelicans,
I cross the wooden
bridge into a cool room
lined with books
and sharp plants.
At first when we wake
from these unmapped places
we are strangers.

Flying high above Laq qui Parle,
above thermals where pelicans
dipped their heads to scan the water,
we didn't speak. What can be said
at those heights? Even pelicans keep
their thoughts to themselves.
I put my hand on your thigh.
We were sardined in that lean cockpit.
It felt good to step out, later,
onto the warm tarmac.

South of the border for a summer,
we fended off history by sucking a lime
bitter and acerbic and by chewing
a clove of garlic raw every day—
a phrophylactic against Montezuma's revenge.

Every few days the van broke down,
on a main street in rain,
behind a whitewashed church.
You shimmied beneath with tools
and a flashlight to make cursed offerings.

A team of marathon runners pushed
the van out of a parking lot on La Bufa
and shouted as we turned a curve down
into Zacatecas, all the windows open
as if to make us bouyant.

Once we camped beside the *zócalo*,
once behind a church, once on a narrow
spit between bay and ocean. At night
we raised the top, crawled
up onto the shallow mattress.

Then we'd wake pressed together,
cows grazing near the driver's door,
or a paleta vendor crossing the avenue beside us,
that once water rose to the tires,
and we could have drowned.

In the year we were born, Fidel
led his corps of earnest men and women

into the future. The revolutionaries
knew something about poetry.

Do you remember the patio where
we listened to Flora sing Cuban *son*

and the owner of the little hotel
where Germans sliced mangoes

into thin bowls showed us a picture
of his grandfather wearing a stiff

collar? We were up late and dancing,
having walked back from *el centro*,

past old women in doorways
and boys kicking a leathery guanabana

as if they were Pele, the air salty
and our skin prickly with the heat.

Some things must be taken a chance on.
We were up late dancing on that patio.

People say things about making love
all night, but I don't believe them.

Later we opened the one window
in our narrow room, above our narrow bed.

The next day we ran our fingers over
the bullet holes in Castro's boat.

You rode all summer on your black
bicycle, 1980, Oregon to D.C.

I collected beautiful words:
chitinous, bezoar, flong

too polished to put in a stanza.
I'd take them out of their

satin hidey-holes and imagine
writing them on your body.

I hoarded them for your return.
Here they are, after all these years,

chiselled beauties—
I never did give them up.

Before we were stopped by cops—a black man humoring
his white partner—on 47th in the ghetto,
we'd been drinking stiff gin and tonics at Theresa's,
blues club with a mural of a lion roaring out
from between a naked woman's spread legs. Late, when all
the other white folks had paid up and gone, a skinny man
old enough to have great-grandchildren and two hobbies
left three floppy-breasted women and whiskey set-ups
and asked me to dance. The blues do not require touching.
A gangly bass man wedged his slow burning cigarette
between D and G, moved his long-boned ringless fingers
soft and patient along the neck. I was a white girl
from a small corn-belt town trying anything.
The old man moved sure from the hips, an easy-does-it
butter-glide. Which of the three women would he lie down
beside later, the three sirens with whiskey 7s
who paid him no mind, nor me either? We danced the blues
oblivious, gone, gone, a slow mojo, and my husband watched
from our back table, gone too, until, two verses in
one of those women called to him to dance and he did,
oh he did, I saw, slow, so slow the blues got him too.

The crazy one inside me wants
to sing to the crazy one inside you—
we'll light candles, hundreds of them
around the tiled salon somewhere
in the foothills of the Hindu Kush
and when we strike the bronze gong
a tattooed old woman will come
with mint tea and a silver plate
of Turkish delight and a little hashish
and she'll stay with us long enough to tell
a winding story about her ancestors,
a story with camels and yurts and
sharp yoghurt laced with the honey
of bees drunk on white anemones.
How the crazy one inside me sings!

When you come knocking
wear anything, a yellow toga
and a gray fedora,
a MacDonald plaid kilt,
plastic bananas strung
along your belt, nothing.
Carry anything, a bouquet
of hothouse lilies, a box
of gem-tone mints, fourteen
lines of Petrarchan lovesickness,
a wren in a bamboo cage.
When you come knocking
be clear-headed, be true,
turn three times on the stoop
and when I open the door
step in as if for the first time.

What I like is to watch you
in the garden. How you stand
before a tomato vine surveying
what has been, what's to come.
How you bend to the weeds
then make a clearing
for snapdragons and mint.
Once you've set the sprinkler
you step back into the rainbow.
And that's it, a summer day,
puddles form in the black soil,
little spoons of cloud among the green.

Swallows carry summer from their tails,
the long advertisement of high sun and fulfillment,
but first they bank and stall in pairs

like hands forming cat's cradle. Clouds fall
through the interstices of wing and beak.
They speak a bird arabic, the swooping letters,

and this should be a ghazal, but beloved,
we can't begin to count the stars or name
the ways the sky calls to us. Pour the wine

and sit here beside me. Somewhere a four-
legged creature stops to smell the leaves and then she
will twine and wait for dark. Beloved, hold me.

Holding hands on a hot day—
like grabbing a fish—
there's so much to learn about love.

❧

Be peony tickled by ant—
I'll be the patient longing of summer

❧

The hollyhock throws
open her sashes—sunshine
and later a bee.

❧

Under one umbrella,
your left shoulder wet,
my right shoulder wet,
we crossed the river.

The moon grabs up
a tiny slice of sky
night after night
until it stares
at us. We are abashed
by its hunger.
Then, night by night,
we take a little
of the moon
into our hearts,
tiny slivers of light
right to our hearts.

On the Sea of Marmara, rust-orange
tankers sloughed water, gulls tripped

against themselves, a commuter train
bound for the Bosporus

passed below our wooden hotel.
We sat on the roof. It was

the gate to paradise. Muezzins
sang into loud speakers

songs tinny and awkward,
several songs braiding above us.

Men in white cotton shirts unbuttoned
to the sternum, men slender as clouds,

hung from open doors to catch relief
in the already hot morning.

No one has witnessed
the lovemaking of hump-backed
whales, the slow caress along
blue flesh, the song
spiralling out toward
sand and wave and seashell
to that small place inside
the conch that gives
up reverberations.

When we hold the shell
or even our cupped hand
against our ear, we hear
the two whales move against
one another as if two
waves had fallen back,
as if an ear and a shell,
two ears, two hands even,
had spiralled inward.

John Cage said that quiet sounds
are like love

a monarch dropped down
into the white snapdragons

one wing sighed away
an arc of silence

returned to the radial
connecting body to light

how I wanted to hear
the powdery meeting of wings

The publisher's most fervent hope is to lubricate the machinery
of social intercourse.

— from the Preface to The Language of Flowers, 1856

Though no flower stands for *fervency,*
the cuckoo plant
     an *idle weed* Lear wore in his madness
     Cardamine pratensis
as *ardor* might do

And there's no flower
for *lubricate*
none for *intercourse*

though a nosegay of whole straw (*union*)
and chickweed (*rendezvous*)
might welcome intercourse,
and for *lubrication*
the vine.

Such a plain bouquet for such *fervent hopes.*

In the fugue of love, something
is always opening. A door
and a duck walks in.
Or maybe it's a solicitor wearing
a trilby. Does it matter? The duck
opens its beak and something expected
comes out and something unexpected.
The solicitor claps and then
opens his briefcase. He knows
the 5-digit code. Out of the red interior
he begins to pull a silk ribbon.
He pulls and pulls. The duck steps
on the ribbon. A flamenco dancer
appears out of nowhere. She opens
her hands and they look like fans.
No, they look like sea anemones.
The solicitor opens his mouth
to say something, but then the duck
flaps its black wings and the flamenco
dancer stamps her feet. A trap door
in the floor opens and everyone
falls through. Love is like that.

Some stand below windows
and long to float,

others sing, slowly at first,
shyly, but in a major key,

still others belt it out, bring down
acorns and pull up oaks,

some throw bombs or sand
or silk scarves or rocks wrapped with verse,

or insults, You Churl! You Suckworm!
or flattering syllables, irridescent and nubby,

others pray, beseech,
demand, repeat themselves,

and one passes without even looking up
all the while imagining

how it will be when the beloved behind the window
comes down.

i

My father took pictures
of my mother
from behind. She'd
bend to grab a baby,
pick berries, not even posing.

ii

1947, Cape Cod, Marlon
went to see Tennessee
about a part, ended up
on his hands and knees
before the kitchen plumbing.
Tennessee swooned.

iii

One summer vacation
my mother followed
a rough farmer
around Fort Ridgely,
his hands so big
he could grab
a woman's ass
and mean it. I was old
enough to know this
was on her mind.

iv

I watch my husband
turn soil,
bend to pick out rocks
and I'm translated
like Puck, fool that I am.

In the pocket of our held hands—
enough energy
to power a tilt-a-whirl!

৵৩

Bright larva in the parsley—
you return it to the garden,
stop to pull a weed.

৵৩

All morning I peeled pears,
carried the slick yellow skin
to the compost. Bees waited.

৵৩

You flew over harrowed fields,
irrigation circles, ditches under water—
just to come home.

৵৩

Frogs on the road—
what direction do I swerve?
How long until I'm in your arms?

In what remained of an Augustinian monastery
south of Zacatecas, just off the Silver Road,
we walked the stations of the cross, beside limestone
porticoes pocked and scarred, a fountain crumbling
in the patio below. We stood in a long corner room
where one gaunt window opened to sere fields
and fences of ocotillo cactus. Commodes of stone
squatted in a row along the outer wall. We spoke
of how Luther wondered at God's love while sitting
on the privy. Some things require solitude. Today,
decades later, I think of that emptied place,
how quiet it was, as if still in meditation, of the red
hollyhocks against a stone ledge, and the swallows
careening across the canted roof. I think of the two
of us, novices in the world, how vivid that memory,
and I am astonished at the mystery of love.

An owl's eye moon
hangs above
the ferris wheel.
Families hold
the earth down.
Teenagers tilt
and blink,
rise arc–wise,
hide their plied
hands. We two
stand below
knowing no one
in the gaudy cars,
but leaning sweet
and salty
with the pleasure
of watching.

Depressed people tend to feel gray rather than blue, whereas people who
are not depressed generally feel yellow.

– from "Findings," *Harper's Magazine*, April 2010

When I'm with you, yellow
becomes green and clouds
skedaddle. When I'm with you
a gypsy band edges out the lone
violinist. They start with
Django and add
pipes and a hurdy-gurdy.
With you everybody who was
sitting stands and we all
do the Hokey Pokey in slow motion.
That's what it's all about!
With you heat lightning circles
the horizon and pocket gophers
line up along the gravel road.
A wind topples the pink flamingoes
and the giggling neighbor girls
set them right. Green becomes red
and the gypsies do the Hokey Pokey
with the violinist. With you
there's heat lightning everywhere,
anything can happen.
With you I'm green, red,
yellow, yellow, yellow.

It is the most ordinary
of affairs. I fold underwear,
you roll out garbage,
I nudge you so you'll roll over,
you nudge me so I'll
stop talking.

You weed the tomatoes,
I arrange the hose
in an oblique S-curve around
mint, basil, cucumbers coming on.
You turn up to a flock
of pelicans high and hushed,
thermal charged,
sunlight on your cheekbones,
your eyes the color of sky.
Thirty years in
and silence has its merits.

The alchemists of love abandoned
heavy metals, inert gas, anything
with a half life. They turned off
the blue flames, let the fridge stand
open all day long, and went outside.

Barefoot they crossed the paddock, climbed
the crooked fence, made for the woods.
We stopped expecting them back
and have only received the one
postcard: *Wish you were here.*

Fall

Some days our love
is a wilderness

here damp with maidenhair ferns
tiny red spiders

oblivious to rain
spongy white mushrooms

leaning drunkenly
against fallen oaks

only the two of us
pretending to be lost

leaving no trail
not cutting our initials

into bark moving easily
toward the deer's path.

One cold morning,
wind against the panes
and rattling the flue,
I woke already tired—

dreams of high water,
of losing a spoon and
crossing a fiery
swamp on a shifting path—

and there you were
beside me, tucked like a beetle
into the blanket,
sweet in your waking.

A rooster crowed,
the wind calmed,
from somewhere across the city
a church bell began to ring.

I thought, when I was twenty, that when I turned
fifty, I'd be immune to love's vicissitudes,
and here I am at fifty, indoors, peeling the skin
of a beet, my fingers bloody seeming, and I'm
watching you outside with our grown daughter,
her back's to me, she could be me, something
about how she leans forward from her shoulders.
All those years ago, what was it we argued about
so fiercely I crossed the Michigan Avenue bridge,
the Wrigley Building white and tranquil behind us,
but we couldn't let it go, couldn't walk away, we
hollered across the traffic. Even now I can feel
my spine lengthen, my shoulders square back,
a little ferocity hardening me. I finish the beets
and lean toward the screen, as if to hear what you
and she say to one another, how you work it out.

We drove across high prairie,
the Mississippi behind us,
nothing ahead for miles
but sky,

a loamy sky, thick enough
to put a trowel into,
but off to the south
clouds pulled

away from one another
as if to stand back
take a long look,
and in that

space what light was left
of the sun
already gone below
the horizon

flowed up and held there
and we did too hold
our breaths at the sudden
beauty.

I walked through the door after a weekend away
hello, hello, and then we were naked
and chanting softly into one another's ears
hello, hello, oh, oh,
and all around the house was quiet,
leaves fell outside the window,
hello, hello, they said as they tilted
this way and that way down to the grass,
down to the last green, down to where
they will nestle and curl and eventually
succumb to the weight of snow,
to where they will leave their bodies
and dissolve into humus and worm,
and one day who knows how long from now
they will dissolve into wing,
they will defy gravity.

The old garter snake had gone in
for the winter, in to his dirt bunker
below the concrete steps. Rhubarb
fell flat against the soil in the night.

Marigolds held up their bright flags
and chrysanthemums stood bold.
Something in their veins is deep,
these stalwarts at the turning season.

We stood together in the kitchen
holding our hot coffee, letting the thin
steam rise to our chins. Beloved,
how strong you are, like the purple mums.

Geese in the disced fields
call in candid voices—
how many ways do we seek one another?

＊

In your arms at dawn—
a train pulls its long whistle—
right through our bodies.

＊

If you were a bird,
you'd be on my life list.

＊

Cockleburrs reach out
as if the world depended
on another's dance.

＊

Fall's grasses come loose—
even the horizon moves
when we move.

In a preface to a book of love
I'd start with the afternoon
my parents raked leaves together
one fall, the maple red as salmon,
elm leaves elegant in the sun's own
vestments, the air stiff with winter
coming on, and my mother
lost her wedding band, so we all
knelt down, our knees in the slight
damp, crouched over the season's
disrobing, and sifted, like the last
of the '49ers, for that one small band
of declaration, and for that half hour
love seemed like something that
required no argument at all, simply
a joining together in the act of discovery.

I saw a farm boy
lean into his Guernsey
his ear on her spine

Any two of us
animals together
easy in our attentions

Offer the world
enough devotion
for a good long time.

Otter was the first lover
propelling herself from the muddy
bank, her back paws flared, her claws
pushing into the soft flesh of earth.

Her whiskers made tiny ripples
along her neck and from her throat
came peeps and sighs of happiness.
She stirred the silt,

mica shone near the surface,
memories of fern and snail,
and the otter flipped and arced,
all time present in her joy.

Give me a simple life, a merry heart.
— N.F.S. Grundtvig

For merriment
bring two of like hearts
ripe as plums
on a September morning

For simplicity
follow the cows across a meadow
flowering clover and honeybees
succumb to reverie

For merriment
double yourselves
eight hands gathering apples
chopping and grinding
passing the ceremonial glass

For simplicity
open the doors
the neighbors will come
with wine and bread

For merriment
find everyone in the kitchen
towels for all
and filigreed spoons
cardamom cloves and hazelnut
loaves hot and primal
honey in the comb
cheese from the old country
an icy bottle brought in from snow
water of life
raise up your glasses
merry hearts
ripe and dear

In fall the maidenhair tree
drops her gold onto the grass,
a thousand gilt fans
stirring the air as they float
toward earth, a thousand
coins layered like fish scales.
Look how their backs rise
in waves when a wind blows.
Ten centuries ago monks
in China began tending
these sacred trees who
make a vow of poverty
every fall and renounce
chastity every spring.
I've tucked gingko leaves
between pages of my notebook.
Two fall out, I return them
to a different place, leaves
between leaves.

In a gully thick with sumac
hunters leave the buck carcass
for coyotes and black crows
to gorge until they drag
their bloated bodies up the ravine
onto the frost-rimed plain.

Filled with venison cutlets
the men ease their sated bellies
against their wives'
soft buttocks and sigh deeply
and say a few words about weather,
about what's happening out there.

The moon waited all afternoon
to make its fat, full-bellied
presence known, to throw down
onto the sleeping world the light
of satisfaction, and then ever so slowly
made its way back to hunger.

If you were a cat
I'd pour you a bowl of milk—
you'd sit in the dish of my lap.

❧

Geese like new lovers
belllies to the current
talking the whole way.

❧

The wind was cold and we were alone.
From across the Kattegat
a mournful whistle.

❧

Pelicans in skeins
above sumac and bluestem
mute as old lovers.

❧

My mushroom heart grows
plump and musty in the night—
dreaming of you.

This is an upright
poem with damp
elms and a crow.

Rainy mornings
are without virtues.
Bach will do.

Something like a maze
with no lid.
Mushrooms burst

through soil
little moist heads
tubercular.

I can hear you
snoring. It sounds
like rain coming on.

When we think to ourselves that we're alone,
we must walk out under the juniper
to where mushrooms like wads of used tissue
or like wobbly ears rise up out of the needle-strewn
soil to declare themselves to the world. They are
damp and cool and they smell of sex.
If they were hands they would applaud.
Standing there, bent slightly at the hips, we breathe
toward the mushrooms, slow breaths of awe,
and in our inhalations come the spores these visitors
from the underworld have let go, trusting in
the possibility that they are not alone, not any more.

Across the ferry's rail we leaned,
our elbows touching, our heels
lifted from the deck.

Small bodies of light
dangled in leisurely rhythm
below the water,
small urges of light
alive in the dim and salty water.

We leaned a long time,
we leaned almost weightless,
lit up by wonder.

We listen to Haydn's Variations
in F Minor, a dark key, though not
consuming, rather the dark
of geese passing in October,
their shadows falling where snow
will insulate spring's iris.
I think of a friend who died
a year ago, how he loved Haydn
and wrote of death and carried books
wherever he went. Hold my hand,
help me among the shadows.

We are born
to sorrow.
Even a leaf
falling, red
or gold, can
bring us to tears.
Indeed, even
a leaf. It falls
where we
stood, and where
we stand
something else
falls, or will
before long.
So hold on
while there's
no wind,
and hold on
after, for even
sorrow can
be borne
when there's love.

One cloud, too thin to stake a claim to cloud-ness,
hung in the high blue sky.

Ah, solitary one, I found myself thinking,
what space is available

to you! Not long before, my beloved
held my face

in his hands, kissed me softly, tasting
the wine we'd been sharing.

And then I was alone, striding across the grass
toward an evening lecture,

already imagining the argument, alive
with ideas, the space

they take up in my head, and that cloud
stopped me, reminded me

that fullness and emptiness, solitude and camaraderie,
need one another.

On his fiftieth birthday, Issa wrote: From now on,
it's all clear profit,
every sky.

What returns
we're destined for!
Waking next to you, morning, morning, morning

and thinking to myself, as I will, another in-the-black
day this will be,
no lop-sided

balance sheet, no dashes like lifebuoys, or red
ink. Instead the sky
wise

and open,
wind, maybe
and us below it, amazed at our good fortune.

Winter

Some say civilization
started with sweets—

after a man chased
the bees from a hive

and carried it back
to the shade beside

a watering hole,
others tarried,

dipped their fingers
into the damp walled

pockets of delight,
and then, sucking

finger by finger
made small talk.

The honey lasted until
stars shot across the firmament,

and some, the hungry ones,
fell to kissing

in case more honey
could be found.

St. Valentine gave up his head
it's said, but not before he'd made
his jailer's daughter see again.

You and I might moralize a bit
on love and vision, but stop:
the truth is we know little

about the martyred saint, Valentino
the Worthy, patron saint of amoré,
he who gave us paper hearts

and doilies and "Be Mine" in sugar
and pink lace and bouquets of
roses trucked north thousands

of lonely miles by heavy-set
men in seed caps who stay in
touch by phone and send postcards

from Truck Stops Hot Showers
All Night Weigh Scale Open
that feature four views of the

interstate exchange. *Missing you.*
Long drive ahead. Sleeping alone.
My head hurts I'm so crazy for you.

Loveland Colorado Loveland Ohio
Loveland Mountain Loveland Pass
       pass through pass over pass into
Lovelock Nevada
       ah to be there
       the key gone missing
Love Point on Chesapeake Bay
       billowing
       passing across
Loves Park near Rockford
       entering at dusk
       in pairs
       here loves there loves
       the steamed windows
       the pressure
Loving a whole county in Texas
       given over to the divine
Lovingston Virginia Lovington New Mexico
       the snakey S
       a whole town misplaced
Lovington where oil wells
       cool two through
       a summer night
Loveland in January
       a taste of bliss

The DJ at KLUV opened
the lines for call-ins,
put on an old tune, something
by Noel Coward,
and waited. He tipped
his chair back, lengthened
his thighs a bit keeping his feet
flat on the floor.
Everyone was home—
snow falling at an angle,
roads icy and impassable,
the windows flecked—
everyone was baking bread
or cracking pecans, or
better yet, sitting on the couch
holding hands.
The DJ sat up straight,
cued Aretha
and danced by himself
in the padded compartment
at the station, where the snow
fell even faster and left
a drift two-thirds up the main door.

You build a blazing fire,
I'll bring dates and pistachios.
Listen! Winter lasts all evening.

ॐ

You rise on a cold morning—
come back so I can melt the world
right off your pimpled and handsome body!

ॐ

You lift knives from soapy water
through flowing water—
I'm ready with a cloth.

ॐ

Frost warning—
let's fill up on brown rice and butter on thick bread,
curl up in one another's arms
for the long dark season.

You turn the iron handle while I
spoon in clods of liver and lumps of fat.
We take turns cranking and spooning
five times, each time the flesh growing
more smooth and purple
and beautiful. How often we have
shared the brave body: lovemaking,
childbirth, the messy offices of raising children.
We put the *leverpostej* into the oven,
wash the iron machine, scrub
circles of blood from the floor.
Then a possum crosses the snowy yard.
We pause in our bloody work to watch him slip
under the over-turned rowboat.
I think his mate, pregnant and waiting,
listens in case something stirs inside.

Another cold and snowy winter, they're saying—
the they who are listened to when they say
such things. Fewer women will vote this year
I read today, and fewer youth. It's okay
to eat egg yolks, to sleep on your back,
okay to touch your friends. Live long enough,
you'll forget more than you'd like. Corn syrup
is just as bad for you as sugar. I'm not afraid.
The cats met me at the door and you're here.

Today you locked your office door
and strolled down the hallway, your shoes
rapping against linoleum, and your colleagues,
still burrowed into their desk chairs, surely thought
to themselves how nice to go home just now, turn
off this light and go on home, who knows if
anyone will be there. But they didn't, you did,
you eased down the stairs, out into the cold
and on the way home you listened to the early news,
stories of mismanagement and distrust. Cows
across the highway blew steam toward the west
and you turned east and then south and you were
home, just like that, and from your chair in the living
room you watched me come through the door.

We spend the morning
at the small tasks

stroking books and hand-thrown pots
with the pink duster

heaving the vacuum cleaner
downstairs and pulling it across carpet

returning books to shelves
and pencils to the drawer

passing one another shoulder
to shoulder noticing what we've done

what's left to do. How satisfying
it is to share the chores

and then to sit with friends
late into the night arguing

about the nature of metaphor
the origins of things.

All day long
I think love
is an abstraction

then a flock
of juncoes
arrives on the deck

to make notes
on the snow
staves of song

in the snow
around cracked corn
and sunflower seeds

and we sit
watching melody
arrive just beyond

the glass and
defying the rules
we hear it.

Here you are now!
Coming through the door,
snow on your ankles.

❦

Thirty years of love—
a tree falling in a wood—
we hear it, or we don't.

❦

Across a crowded room
I saw you seeing me—
even now I blush.

❦

Hold a pear to your lips—
sun, earth, water—
another flourishing.

❦

You, reader, write your own
poem of love. Leave it in a silk pocket
for someone like you to find.

Bitter cold
frost scree on the windows
sun searing its mark
on the landscape

ah now I sit
at the black piano
to play Satie
waves of sound

simple and round
not too proud
slow and grave
bury the sound

outside you move
snow as if this
is the most natural
thing in winter

inside I'm hearing
that far off wind
Satie heard on his
walks from Paris

come inside love
slow and grave
put your hand just
here for the pulse

Between Cyrus and Chokio a flock of snow geese
rested on water standing
in a barren field. The sky was pink beyond them
and striped in soft clouds.
The whole landscape seemed contained by the mute
colors of dusk, colors
of animals who live in the open, who poke their noses
into the spaces tractors make,
who lift their heads as children do after a long time spent
looking at a bug.
This time of year, after the snow has melted but before
buds stick their necks out,
this is the contemplative time of year as when twenty years ago
we felt a child kick
inside me, took turns caressing the thick place where her foot
prodded the world.

On Super Bowl Sunday snow falls thick
and wet, heavy pads of it weighing down
the pines' shoulders. Friends gather
in other houses, but in ours I huddle
at my desk scratching lines of love
on a blank page, the door to my study open
to where my husband sits alone watching
the slow grind of time outs, reading the news
during commercials, cracking nuts while the ball,
wobbling only a little like a comet, sails
over astroturf. In a college writing class,
where we met years ago, I wrote an essay,
"Football as a Metaphor for Life." He laughed
at me—my future husband. I knew more then
about the game. First down by first down
snow piles up in the streets. When the game ends,
friends part, drive home, their rear tires sliding
across ruts of snow, windshield wipers
thwapping this way and that way
making visible all that whiteness.

I could learn from Hafiz, I think—
something about the divine—

but now let's sit here in winter dusk
and read, so quiet we can hear

the cat licking his haunches. Soon
we'll look up and find one another

across the rug, in this room of windows,
as if we'd been apart for months.

When I am playing the piano
and you are in the other room
I know you are not reading
though you hold a book open
and I think, if I were Liszt I'd throw
you something—white gloves
or a half-smoked cigar—that you'd
save in a secret place and take out
once or twice a year. The ear is
a secret place and I have nothing
to toss you but this ragged music.

Hours before we rise
the blue moon eases past.

Now my body doesn't ebb
and flow. How warm

you are beside me
this chill morning.

I'll read something propitious
into these two December moons:

one moon a blessing
for all that has passed,

the second a smooth bone
thrown high into the night,

thrown so that we might
divine what's to come.

At dinner with friends
we talked of burial,
of what we'd want done
with our bodies

of how worms
could enter our cavity
and carry us away
as molecules

or perhaps how
being laid out on
a platform so that
ravens and buzzards

might feast on us
how that could be
the right thing, to lie
below the clouds

in some sacred place
that's what we wanted
to be placed somewhere
holy and then we cut

into pheasant breasts
and crusty bread
and we lifted our glasses
to toast this life

we two couples
children grown
rejoicing in our long
loves and looking forward

snow falling lightly
onto the road
traffic moving past
slowly, slowly

I find that I cannot
say a last poem about love.

There's an oatmeal sky today,
churlish, sodden.

The cat went out, tiptoed
across the windowsill,

his five circled prints
delicate violet petals.

Beloved, you'll have
to shovel the snow,

I'll bake the dense rye
that goes with leverpostej.

No one else around here
likes it the way we do.

We could lie down later
for a nap with the cats.

We don't have to make
anything of the day, this time

together, these years. Look,
beloved, a robin at the feeder.

Index of First Lines

ABOUT THE AUTHOR

Athena Kildegaard is a lecturer at the University of Minnesota, Morris. Her previous books of poetry are *Rare Momentum* and *Bodies of Light*, both from Red Dragonfly Press. She has received the LRAC/McKnight Fellowship and grants from the Lake Region Arts Council and the Minnesota State Arts Board. *Cloves & Honey* is the culmination of a year of writing a love poem every day—a daunting but also deeply satisfying project.